Numbers on the Move

1 2 3
Dance and Count with Me

Written by

Teresa Benzwie, Ed.D.

Illustrated by Mark Weber

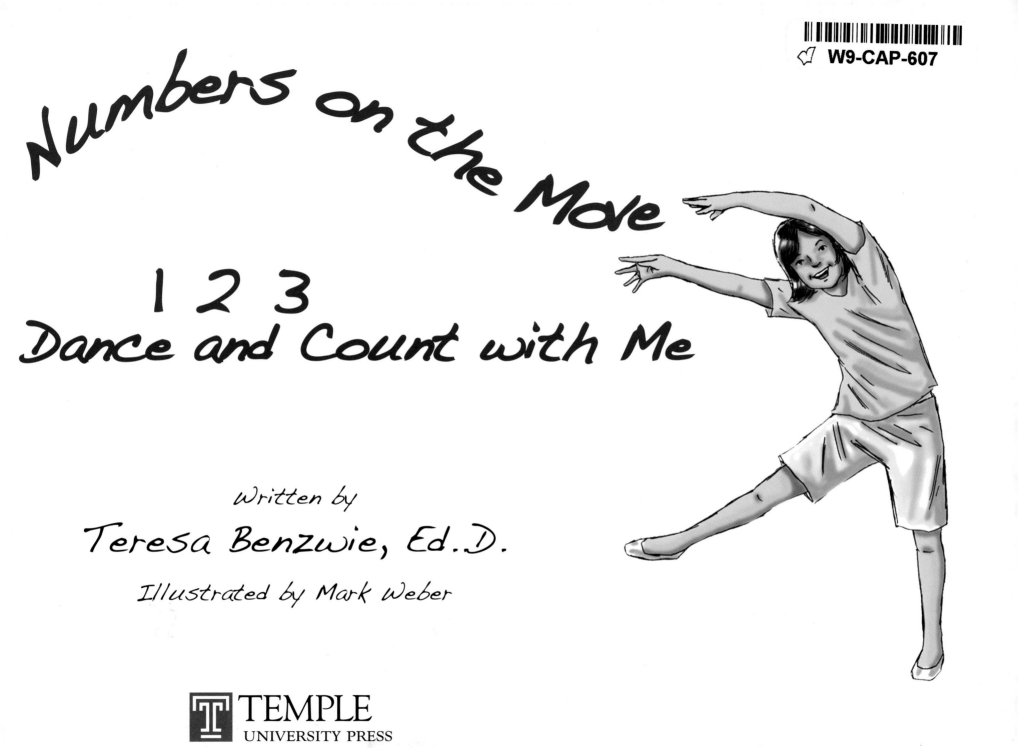

T TEMPLE
UNIVERSITY PRESS

This book is dedicated with deep appreciation to:

Edrie Ferdon, Ph.D., doctoral advisor, whose vision, unconditional regard and wisdom launched my dance career.
Marcia Prager, my beloved rabbi, who nurtured and guided the spirit within while sharing her unbounded creativity.
Edwin Castillo, M.D., mentor and colleague, who inspired and supported the beginning of my adventures as a psychotherapist.

And my precious grandchildren, **Briana – Sophia – Ellis – Violet – Misha – Merci**

Many friends and colleagues have contributed their time, energy and creative ideas. Deep gratitude and many thanks go to:

Rabbi Marcia Prager, Harlene Galen, Ed.D. and Rima Faber, Ph.D., for untold hours of inspiration, creative expertise and love poured into this book.

Mick Gusinde-Duffy, Senior Acquisitions Editor at Temple University Press, whose steadfast patience and belief in this project brought *Numbers on the Move* home.

Robert Bender for his love, creative support and energies.

Wendy Verna, Designer, and Mark Weber, Illustrator, for their flexibility and imagination in making this book dance. Michael DiMotta for final illustrative touches grounding the dancing children throughout the book and cover.

A big thank-you also goes to: Charles Ault, Production Director, and David Wilson, Production Coordinator, at Temple University Press, Lawrence Bender, Jody Folk, Christina Bothwell, Siri Weber Feeney, Sheila Greenberg, Donna Scott, Sarah Hilsendager, Craig Bender, Anita Misrachi, Sara Misrachi, Liz Albert and Elizabeth Bender for all their encouragement and creative contributions.

I also thank the Temple University Press staff for their support in all aspects of the book's publication.

TEMPLE UNIVERSITY PRESS
Philadelphia, Pennsylvania 19122
www.temple.edu/tempress

Copyright © 2011 by Teresa Benzwie
All rights reserved
Published 2011

Library of Congress Cataloging-in-Publication Data

Benzwie, Teresa.
    Numbers on the move / Teresa Benzwie.
        p. cm.
    ISBN 978-1-4399-0342-1 (pbk.) – ISBN 978-1-4399-0343-8 (e-book)
    1. Counting–Juvenile literature. 2. Dance–Juvenile literature.
I. Title.
    QA113.B46 2011+
    513.211–dc22
                                            2010049039

This book is printed on acid-free paper for greater strength and durability.

Manufactured in China by C&C Offset Printing Co. Ltd.
Shenzhen, Guangdong Province
Printed in February 2011

2 4 6 8 9 7 5 3 1

Zero

0

Zero means none
Nothing to do

This is a quiet time
for every part of you

1

One Stretch

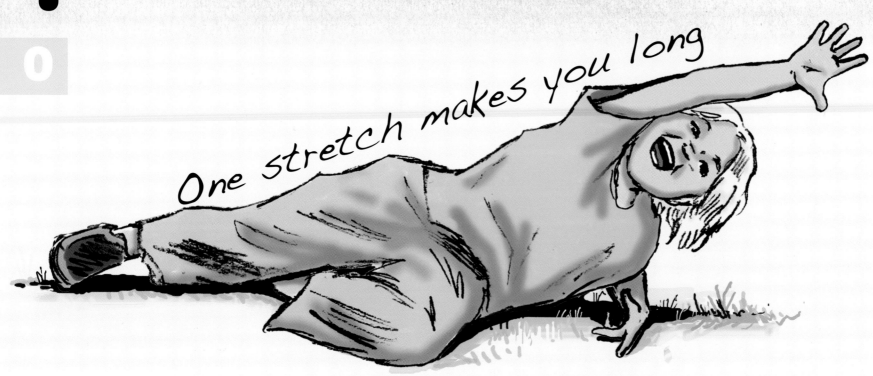

One stretch makes you long

Makes you tall
Makes you strong

**Stretch again to one
Have fun!**

Two Slides

Two slides are easy to do

First by myself

and then with you

Can you try something new with two?

Three Jumps

3

How else can you jump with three?
Let me see!

Four Kicks

Kick high   with left and right

and all
your
might

Kick
with
Joy

Can you kick more with four?

Five Walks

*Walk with five
and come alive!*

**Walk your own way to five
Step and jive!**

Six Twists

6

Six twists
with
legs
arms
and wrists

5
4
3
2
1
0

What else can you twist with six?

Eight Marches

8

March eight times in a row

Change directions

as you go!

7
6
5
4
3
2
1
0

You march great to number eight!

9

Nine

8
7
6
5
4
3
2
1
0

Nine times to hop

Hops

9

Count nine then stop

8
7
6
5
4
3
2
1
0

Changing feet that's okay
You can hop to nine any way!

10

9
8
7
6
5
4
3
2
1
0

Clap your hands high in the air

Claps

Clap to ten anywhere

9
8
7
6
5
4
3
2
1
0

**Hooray for you! You've clapped to ten!
Can you clap to ten again?**

Moving up to ten is fun

1 One

2 Two

3 Three

4 Four

5 Five

The Rhythm of Your Name

How many beats are in your name?
James that's One
So-phie Two
Po-lin-a Three
A-lex-an-der Four
Show me more

I count each sound
in my name
When I say yours
I do the same

Dance your name
around the room
Zoom!

Counting Numbers

Move with the numbers   Count to the beat
Clap your hands   Tap your feet
Count one two three four with your

Head
    Shoulders
        Elbows
            Hands
                Arms
                    Hips
                        Knees
                          Feet

Can you stop when you are done?
Even when you're having fun?

0

0
Zero

Zero is a place of rest
Now you know
you've done your best

Breathe in deep
Breathe out slow
Feel your mind and body
grow
grow
grow

1

One

2
Two

1
One

3

3
Three

2
Two

1
One

2
1
0

4

3
2
1
0

4
Four

3
Three

2
Two

1
One

5

4
3
2
1
0

5
Five

4
Four

3
Three

2
Two

1
One

6

5
4
3
2
1
0

6 Six

5 Five

4 Four

3 Three

2 Two

1 One

7

6
5
4
3
2
1
0

4
Four

5
Five

3
Three

2
Two

1
One

6
Six

7
Seven

9

8

7

6

5

4

3

2

1

0

3 Three

4 Four

2 Two

1 One

You will be a counting hero!

10

5 Five

4 Four

3 Three

2 Two

1 One

9
8
7
6
5
4
3
2
1
0

10

9
8
7
6
5
4
3
2
1
0

When you count down from ten to zero

10
Ten

9
Nine

8
Eight

7
Seven

6
Six

But look!
Our counting book's not done!

6
Six

7
Seven

8
Eight

9
Nine

10
Ten